MAKE RACISTS AFRAID AGAIN

Title: Make Racists Afraid Again
ISBN-13: 978-1-942825-14-2
Author: Kambiz Mostofizadeh
Publisher: Mikazuki Publishing House

Description: Make Racists Afraid Again is about the rise of Fascism in America and how you can fight against it.

Like us on Facebook
Facebook.com/KambizMostofizadeh

MAKE RACISTS AFRAID AGAIN

TABLE OF CONTENTS

MAKE RACISTS AFRAID AGAIN

STOP THE EXCUSES

According to a newsletter titled "Fascism!" from Army Talk Orientation Fact Sheet 64 by the U.S Defense Department from March 24th 1945, "Fascism is government by the few and for the few. The objective is seizure and control of the economic, political, social, and cultural life of the state. Why? The democratic way of life interferes with their methods and desires for: (1) conducting business; (2) living with their fellow-men; (3) having the final say in matters concerning others, as well as themselves. The basic principles of democracy stand in the way of their desires; hence democracy must go! Anyone who is not a member of their inner gang has to do what he's told. They permit no civil liberties, no equality before the law. They make their own rules and change them when they choose. They maintain themselves in power by use of force combined with propaganda based on primitive ideas of "blood" and "race," by skillful manipulation of fear and hate, and by false promise of security. The propaganda glorifies war and insists it is smart and "realistic" to be pitiless and violent. Any fascist attempt to gain power in America would not use the exact Hitler pattern. It would work under the guise of "super-patriotism" and "super-Americanism." Fascist leaders are neither stupid nor naive. They know that they must hand out a line that "sells." Huey Long is said to have remarked that if fascism came to America, it would be on a program

MAKE RACISTS AFRAID AGAIN

of Americanism. Fascists in America may differ slightly from fascists in other countries, but there are a number of attitudes and practices that they have in common.

1. Pitting of religious, racial, and economic groups against one another in order to break down national unity is a device of the "divide and conquer" technique used by Hitler to gain power in Germany and in other countries. With slight variations, to suit local conditions, fascists everywhere have used this Hitler method. In many countries, anti-Semitism (hatred of Jews) is a dominant device of fascism. In the United States, native fascists have often been anti-Catholic, anti-Jew, anti-Negro, anti-Labor, anti- foreign-

born. Interwoven with the "master race" theory of fascism is a well-planned "hate campaign" against minority races, religions, and other groups. To suit their particular needs and aims, fascists will use any one or a combination of such groups as a convenient scapegoat.

2. Fascism cannot tolerate such religious and ethical concepts as the "brotherhood of man." Fascists deny the need for international cooperation. These ideas contradict the fascist theory of the "master race." The brotherhood of man implies that all people regardless of color, race, creed, or nationality **have rights."**

MAKE RACISTS AFRAID AGAIN

Everyone tries to come up with reasons for Trump's victory. Russia. Rising angry White Middle Class. Alex Jones. Every reason is stated except the obvious which is that America has always been a White Supremacist Ultra-Nationalistic oppressive warmongering Empire. Out of the past 240 years, America has been at war for 224 years. America has always thought of itself as being "Chosen" and "Special" in the eyes of God. Americans belief in their own Exceptionalism is programmed and ingrained deeply in the American psyche. Liberal Americans and Conservative Americans are two sides of the same coin, one is less Liberal and one is more Liberal. Both of them love their Flag and both of them recite

MAKE RACISTS AFRAID AGAIN

Nationalistic mantras. Republicans say "Make America Great Again" and Democrats/Liberals say "America was Already Great". NO!!!!! America was NEVER GREAT. Say it again. America was never great. Americans are responsible for the Murder of 100 Million Native Americans, 20 Million African Americans, and millions of Muslims in the Middle East. America was never great. America was always evil and vile because of what it did. American Exceptionalism is really a statement that the world is lacking in sophistication and Americans are the culture bearers bringing light to the heathens of the world. But what about President Obama, was he not Anti-Colonial? President Obama is responsible for the creation of tens of millions of refugees in the Middle East. It does not matter if you are Black, Brown, White, Green, Yellow, Orange, Magenta, Cyan, or Crimson Red. If you support the continuation of War policies while mouthing off Liberal ideals, then you are a Progressive Fascist. President Obama was serving his White Supremacist masters when he invaded Iraq, Afghanistan, and Libya. President Obama was serving his White Supremacist masters when he ordered dropping bombs in Syria. Your color, creed, religion, belief system, race, or ideology are irrelevant. It is what you do that matters, not what you say. Trump is just continuing the White Supremacy which Obama handed off to him. You don't have to be a Neo-Nazi or Blond

or White to be a White Supremacist.
If you have ever said "America is the
greatest nation on earth" then you
are a White Supremacist. If you have
ever said "America has the greatest
military on earth" then you are a
Fascist. America was never great.
America was always White
Supremacist and minorities like
African-Americans have been a key
player in propping up and supporting
White Supremacism in America by
following the same oppressive and
ultra-nationalistic views that their
former slave masters carry.

According to a documented study
and analysis of Fascism in Europe
that was prepared in 1947 at the
instance and under the direction of
Representative Wright Patman of

10

MAKE RACISTS AFRAID AGAIN

Texas by Legislative Reference Service of the Library of Congress, Fascist movements have these elements:

1. The wiping out of all independent trade-unionism with the result that those trade-unions which are permitted, exist only under the tolerance of the totalitarian state, to serve as its servile adjuncts.

2. The elimination of political parties except the ruling Party.

3. The subordination of all economic and social life to the strict control of the ruling, single-party bureaucracy.

4. The suppression of individual initiative, and the liquidation of the system of free enterprise, and a

tendency toward government control of super cartels.

5. The abolition of the right to freedom of speech, press, assembly, and worship.

6. The reduction of wages and living standards.

7. The use of slave labor on a vast scale and the establishment of concentration camps.

8. The abolition of the right to trial by jury, habeas corpus, the right to independent defense counsel, and the innocence of the defendant until proven guilty.

9. The glorification of an all-powerful ruler who is subject neither to criticism nor removal through the ballot.

10. The utilization of a special form of social demagogy for example incitement of race against race and class against class the elimination of all opposition, and the concentration of power into the hands of the ruling dictatorship.

11. The subordination of all economic and social life and the everyday needs of the population to the requirements of an expanding military machine seeking world conquest.

12. The establishment of a system of Nation-wide espionage to which the entire population is subject.

13. The severance of social, cultural, and economic contact between the people of the totalitarian state and those of other countries, through a rigorous press and radio censorship, travel restrictions, etc.

14. The open disregard for the rights of other nations and the sanctity of treaties.

MAKE RACISTS AFRAID AGAIN

WHEN THEY CAME

The European refugees and immigrants that arrived to America in the 1800's and early 1900's faced deep levels of Racism. Polish were ridiculed with jokes and given the worst jobs. Chinese faced extreme levels of racism while they worked building the railroads in California and mining for Gold during the mid-1800's. The Chinese long work ethic and dedication made them hated and despised. Italians were made fun of and degraded with racist nicknames by Nativist (America First) types. Anyone Catholic was viewed with suspicion and seen as a possible agent of the Pope. Every new immigrant group that arrived in America faced ridicule and verbal (and sometimes physical) degradation. As immigrants would get off the boat in to America, they were pelted with scraps of animal meat and rotten vegetables. Immigrants were titled "Fresh off the boat" and degraded verbally with jokes. Immigrants had to fight through the Racism and bigotry that they faced. Immigrants were not welcomed and had to undergo intensely difficult conditions in America to survive the chaotic and harsh pioneer-like environment. As immigrants began to grow richer, Racism increased against them because of their dedicated work ethic and resourcefulness in the face of oppression. Street fights between immigrants' groups and anti-immigration groups was a reality in both the 1800's and 1900's.

MAKE RACISTS AFRAID AGAIN

Immigrants were viewed as evil, not able to be assimilated, and corrupt. This image was pushed by anti-immigration groups who veered towards a Nativist policy that excluded anyone that was not White and Protestant. Cultural superiority and ethnic superiority was based around the premise that White Protestants represented the peak in sophistication. How sophisticated can you be if you killed 100 million Native Americans and 20 million African Americans to take over a land mass? Sophistication comes about through avoiding the brutalities that are created by war. Diplomacy, negotiation, and dialogue shows sophistication and military conflict shows brutality and crude-ness. A nation like the United States that has

been spent the last 224 years out of
the past 240 years in war needs re-
evaluation. You cannot claim to have
any type of moral high ground when
history has shown the opposite of
this. Let us ask the 100 million
Native Americans that were
murdered if the U.S. Government
has the moral high ground. Let us
ask the 20 million African Americans
that were murdered if there is any
type of moral high ground. To claim
a moral high ground there has to be
some type of consistency in the
demonstration of it.

MAKE RACISTS AFRAID AGAIN

SPEAK ONLY ENGLISH?

What is the English language? How did it come about and who framed the modern version that we are using today? White Supremacists in America are quick to point out that only English should be spoken. That would be fine if English was not a fusion language. English is itself a language comprised of French words and German words. In addition, English incorporates and uses Italian, Chinese, Mexican, Arabic, Persian, Indian, African, Japanese, Spanish, and Russian words. English is mostly German (Old English) and French words (which were reserved for the Ruling Classes). Words such as "buy" which are mono-syllabic came in to the English language from German and were reserved for the poor. Words like "purchase" which have more than one syllable were thought of as noble and reserved for the Ruling Classes. White Supremacists have gone so far as to post signs on their businesses stating "English Only!" but never took time to research what the English language is. The English language is an Evolving Language because it is constructed of words from other languages. Additionally, even if individuals have zero allegiance to White Supremacism, the insistence by many that English be the lingua franca or bridge language between cultures, is itself exhibiting White Supremacism.

MAKE RACISTS AFRAID AGAIN

FASCISM IS HISTORICAL

According to the book "Facts and Fascism" by George Seldes, Hitler promised the miserable people of Germany:

1. The abolition of all unearned incomes.

2. The end of interest slavery. This was aimed against all bankers, not only Jewish bankers.

3. Nationalization of all joint-stock companies. This meant The Big Money and Big Profits in Fascism the end of all private industry, not only the monopolies but all big business.

4. Participation of the workers in the profits of all corporations-the mill, mine, factory, industrial worker was to become a part owner of industry.

5. Establishment of a sound middle class. Nazism, like Italian Fascism, made a great appeal to the middle class, the small business man, the millions caught between the millstones of Big Business and labor. The big department stores, for example, were to be smashed. This promise delighted every small shopkeeper in Germany. Bernard Shaw once said that Britain was a nation of shopkeepers. This was just as true for Germany and German shopkeepers were more alive politically. They were for Hitler's Nazism to a man and they supplied a

large number of his murderous S.S. and S.A. troops.

6. Death penalty for usurers and profiteers.

7. Distinction between "raffendes" and "schaffendes" capital between predatory and creative capital. This was the Gregor Strasser thesis: that there were two kinds of money, usury and profiteering money on one hand, and creative money on the other, and that the former had to be eliminated. Naturally all money-owners who invested in the Nazi Party were listed as creative capitalists, whereas the Jews (some of whom incidentally invested in Hitler) and all who opposed Hitler were listed as exploiters.

MAKE RACISTS AFRAID AGAIN

THEY HAVE UNITED

There is no such thing as White
Americans. There are European
Americans that like to believe they
are White, however White is not a
classification for a race. Color is an
antiquated and outdated Western
way of addressing race. If a person
says they are Italian-American, that
does not make them White (except
in their mind) because there are
Italians in Sicily that are as dark as
the darkest African. The so-called
White people of America, unless
they are able to clearly follow their
blood line, are a mix of multiple
races and unless they have a DNA
test done, there is no clear answer
as to what they are. The whole idea
of race science is racist and
supremacist in its essence. It was

created to institutionalize racism.
The so-called White people of
America are not Caucasian however
as they like to believe they are. They
have nothing in common with the
people of the Caucus Mountains,
neither culturally or racially. The
(wildly delusional) White
Supremacists are living in a fictional
fantasy world where humans should
be entitled based on their skin color.
If you want to survive the Fascists,
then you have to understand them.
Many of the Trump Republicans who
also happen to be White
Supremacists and Neo-Nazis openly
talk about the "Final Solution",
referring to White Supremacists goal
of killing all Jewish people on earth.
They also talk about an upcoming
Race War and they express their

wish to see the Race War come about faster. You could imagine a White Supremacist's face with his eyes closed in a reflective pose, personifying a so-called Race War in his mind as he smiles. They think of this hypothetical Race War to come as the event that will allow them to rid the United States of immigrants, Gays, Muslims, undesirables, and anyone not conforming to their Fascist vision. Do you want to hold logical debates with these people? Do you want to reason with them? Good luck. Not only will you gain no traction in argument with them, but you will also be targeted now by their community to be trolled and harassed. You have to shut down wherever they meet and you have to disrupt wherever they gather. Book clubs are the cover that the White Nationalists use on social media websites. Because their websites are monitored, they never say anything that would amount to committing violence against others. But they do post many memes that do so and they openly use derogatory and antiquated terminology when referring to Black Americans and they purposefully misspell and misquote Islamic sayings and words in order to further their cause. The White Nationalists openly use the Swastika to display their hate and they refer to America as ZOG or Zionist Occupied Government. They sell conspiracy theories related to the outrageous White Genocide conspiracy theory and talk about the destruction of Western (White)

MAKE RACISTS AFRAID AGAIN

culture via the corrupting influence of foreigners. They use social media to meet each other offline in a social setting like bars. They display pictures of the demographics of the areas they will meet and decide where to meet based on the racial makeup of the area. Their numbers are increasing as the normalization of hate is allowed by both Conservative and Liberal media outlets.

The Liberals think that chanting slogans, writing articles, and making really good signs, will make the Fascists go away. History has taught us that the Fascists do not go away, but rather the Fascists make everyone that does not look like them go away. If you want to seriously oppose Fascism, then you have to deny the political space online to organize and you have to deny them the political space offline to meet. Liberals try to debate White Supremacists/Neo-Nazi's in order to defeat them with words. First thing I can tell you is words have never defeated a Fascist. But let us entertain the idea of giving Fascists a platform to debate them. How will that help us defeat them? It will only allow the Fascists to have more political space to spread their Hate Speech. By giving them the political space or platform to gain a wider audience, we are in fact helping them grow. Does that mean that exposing them helps them grow? No because exposing them implies that it is a one sided presentation not a two sided debate with a Fascist/Neo-

MAKE RACISTS AFRAID AGAIN

Nazi/White Supremacist. First off, they are Dogmatic and Rigid in their conditioned and pre-programmed belief system that guides their ideology. If you allow them to gain a wider audience, you are helping them and acting in a self-defeating manner. You can't debate a Fascist because a debate implies an interactive exchange in communication. A debate with a Fascist is anything but interactive because they regurgitate memorized Talking Points. This makes debate useless and counter-productive. You have to shut down their place of meeting, shut down their offices, and shut down their rallies. This is how you defeat Fascism. Words alone, I'm afraid, will not go very far. Liberals like Bill Maher represent the problem with the Regressive Left. They are willing to support Liberal ideals but are unwilling to defend Muslim-Americans. They are willing to support Democratic ideals but become unwilling to defend Women's rights. They move Left on issues that matter to them and move right on issues such as Defense. Bernie Sanders was notorious for being the Hero of the Liberals while simultaneously calling for a "Strong Military". Bill Maher has become famous by championing Liberal ideals while simultaneously attacking Muslim ideals and Islamic values. It is a case of having your cake and eating it too. The myth of the Moderate is as false as the Nationalistic Liberal. Progressive Fascist is a better term for a person with Liberal ideals but is also Pro-Military. How can you be a Liberal if you are Nationalistic and Patriotic? Nationalism and Patriotism lead to Xenophobia (hate of foreign nationals). America First is really a coded phrase that tells everyone that either they assimilate in to an "Ethno-State" or leave. Liberals want to appease Fascists with the hope that it will allow their own survival. Appeasing a Fascist is dangerous to delay your own demise. The Fascist may not come for you today but the Fascist can and will come for you the day you stop appeasing them. The White Supremacists organizations, the Alt-Right, and Neo-Nazi organizations are working together. From the United States to England to France to Greece to Germany. What

MAKE RACISTS AFRAID AGAIN

is being witnessed is an organization
that has never happened before.
Racism is normalized, immigrants
are degraded by the establishment
and labeled as criminals, houses of
worship like Synagogues and
Mosques are threatened, vandalized,
shot up, Islamophobia is rampant,
Anti-Semitism is rampant, Sexism is
rampant, the Fascists speak of
"freedom" while invading your
privacy online and offline, Hate
speech is open and allowed, and
militarism (as witnessed in DAPL) is
glorified and celebrated, Hate crimes
are up by exponential numbers,
Mexican-Americans are treated like
2nd class Citizens, Muslim-
Americans are treated like 2nd class
Citizens, and violence against Black
Americans (as well as other

minorities) by Police has increased
substantially. The Fascists have
united and will keep getting more
united. The Liberals in America are
unable to oppose them. The Liberals
in America feel that by just chanting
slogans in the face of Fascism, they
can make a real and permanent
difference. The only way to confront
a Fascist is with the only language
they understand. Fascists use force
to harm humans. Fascism can also
be called Anti-Humanism, because
the enemy are humans and
humankind. Anti-Fascists have to
speak to Fascists in the only
language they understand and that is
force. With force, the Fascists will be
denied a Political Space to spew
their Hate Speech. There are Neo-
Nazi/White Supremacist groups

propping up everywhere. In the
St.Louis, Missouri area there are at
least 19 Neo-Nazi/White
Supremacist Hate Groups that have
been documented with names such
as the Confederate White Knights,
Klu Klos Knights, Militant Knights,
Aryan Nations Sadistic Souls, Aryan
Strikeforce, The Daily Stormer,
American Vanguard, Conservative
Citizens Foundation, St Louis
League of the South, Southern
National Congress, Invictus Books,
and Church of Israel. All of these
groups are supporters and
proponents of the White Supremacist
ideology. In early January 2017, an
83-year-old Korean woman was
attacked in Los Angeles by a
Mexican-American woman yelling
"White Power". The Mexican-

MAKE RACISTS AFRAID AGAIN

American woman who was eventually arrested, was yelling "White Power" as she was attacking an 83-year-old Korean woman. It seems that minorities are just as susceptible to propaganda as the rest of the population is. The Muslim Travel Ban initiated by Trump also had adverse effects on the United States. In February 2017, two hard working Indian engineers in Kansas that worked for GPS company Garmin, Srinivas Kuchibhotla and Alok Madasani, were shot and killed by a White Supremacist named Adam Purinton. Purinton thought the two Indian engineers were Iranian. A bartender working at the Applebee's where Purinton was arrested said "He (Purinton) said he shot and killed two Iranian people in Olathe." When

MAKE RACISTS AFRAID AGAIN

the President of the United States
(POTUS) scapegoats Muslims in
order to win political points with his
White Supremacist/Neo-Nazi
followers, the POTUS is openly
promoting Hate against Muslim-
Americans. Hate Speech leads to
Hate Crime, as has been witnessed
in the past few months. Over 1,000
Hate Crimes in the 1st month of the
Trump regime alone with every
indicator showing increase via the
normalization of hate." Racism is
institutional because Racism is
created by Nationalism. The Nation-
State, for its own survival, tries to
create a unified way of thinking and
unified way of acting, in order to
create national unity. This
Nationalism which guides the new
citizen/resident is based around the

premise that the majority of individuals in that nation-state are from one homogenous race. The entry of immigrants creates a threat to the Nationalism which the Status Quo has architected. Immigrants bring in new ideas, new cultures, new modes of thinking, new products, and new visions (which lead to achievement). The Nation-State attempts to regulate the problem away while simultaneously pushing the promotion of homogeneity (sameness). When the immigrants begin to grow richer than the citizens that existed in the same land before them, the immigrants become scapegoated (blamed for all the problems of society). Nationalism grew out of a need to establish exclusivity. Nationalism is Racist in

MAKE RACISTS AFRAID AGAIN

its essence because Nationalism promotes the importance of the current citizen/residents (Nativist movement of America First) over the needs of immigrants. Immigrants are relegated to a 2nd class citizen along other minorities. Then immigrants have to assimilate or become outsiders in the place they reside. Nationalism, when coupled with notions of "White Survival" and "White Genocide", lead to minorities embracing Racism against immigrants. The media affects how the people seeing the media will view others. The greater the amount of propaganda that is pushed against Muslim-Americans by the media, Hollywood, online social media, and TV shows (like 24 and Homeland), the greater the likelihood that

MAKE RACISTS AFRAID AGAIN

Muslim-Americans (and other minorities like them that are also marginalized) will be further denied the benefits and privileges of living in a society. Marginalization of one or two or three races is absolutely not conducive to creating an environment that is welcoming and inclusive. Nationalism and patriotism promote the marginalization of certain peoples while promoting and prioritizing others. This why Nationalism is not relevant to the current time. Nationalism and patriotism create levels specifically because they systematically prioritize one or two races. Getting rid of marginalization is not an overnight effort but rather a continual program with lengthy process involved. The eradication of marginalization will allow for greater national unity and will help to eradicate problems such as crime and health issues related to its existence. Marginalization is itself a form of Hate Crime that should be outlawed and fought against. Marginalization has short term effects that are known and visible but what about the long term effects of marginalization? Long term marginalization could lead to worse problems than just crime and health issues. Marginalization should be fought against in all forms in order to prevent is side effects from affecting the community.

MAKE RACISTS AFRAID AGAIN

SWEDEN

Who would have thought that
Sweden would become a major
player in the global promotion of
White Supremacism? Sweden is
quickly becoming a hotbed of Anti-
Immigration and Pro-Nationalism
sentiment aimed at Muslim migrants.
Sweden is used as a point of
reference by White Supremacists
and White Nationalists to exhibit the
extent that Western civilization is
experiencing a so-called "Muslim
invasion". The White Supremacists
refer to the entry of Muslims in to
Europe as a hostile invasion that
seeks to get rid of European culture.
Not only is this completely un-true,
but it is conspiratorial in its view.
Swedish mining millionaire Daniel
Friberg has been a major player in

the Alt-Right movement globally,
focusing on shaping and molding the
global political environment with his
White Supremacism from the top
down. Whether it be through the
funding of Fascist publishing house
Arktos with Editor Jason Reza
Jorjani or through the creation of
think tanks, Jorjani (Gorgani is the
probable real name) is the Editor In
Chief of the top Alt-Right (White
Supremacist) publishing house in the
world named Arktos (funded by
Swedish mining millionaire Daniel
Friberg). Jorjani gives speeches
about Iranians experiencing White
Genocide at the hands of invaders
like Arabs. White Genocide? Sure
there are White people in Iran but if
you took a DNA test from each
Iranian, you would find things like

MAKE RACISTS AFRAID AGAIN

Elamite blood (African and Persian mixed), Chinese blood (Asian), Jewish blood (Jews have lived in Iran for thousands of years and thus they have intermarried and intermingled with Iranians for thousands of years), Arab blood (Arabs that live in Iran and celebrate Iranian culture are no less Iranian than anybody else), and African blood (there are at least 2 million African-Iranians living in Iran right now). This whole idea of Race Science and Eugenics is at its core Racist and Supremacist. It is used to create divisions and levels on which the Status Quo can rule. Jorjani's White Genocide cries are just another attempt by White Supremacists to justify their twisted and antiquated racist ideology.

44

MAKE RACISTS AFRAID AGAIN

Friberg has played a major role in pushing the Alt-Right agenda. With the launch of Red Ice TV, the Alt Right is taking an open meta-politics approach to political change. They (mostly all but not all) refer to themselves as White Europeans, tout the Jewish conspiracy of world domination, and see people like Hate Speaker Milo Yiannopolous as being too Liberal. They see Milo as not being completely Alt-Right because he does not promote the White identity agenda. White Supremacist Lana Lokteff said "Once the shock values worn off, he (Milo) will probably find something else because he won't go for 14/88 (a reference to the 14 words of White Supremacists and 88 symbolizing Heil Hitler). White Supremacists like

beautiful Lana Lokteff are being used
to soften the image of Fascism and
to bring Fascism in to the 21st
century with a smiling face. The
softer the face that is placed on
Fascism, the easier it is to sell. In the
United States, the White
Supremacists/Neo-Nazis/Fascists
are hidden or at least attempt to not
bring their Racism in to the open out
of a need for self-preservation. Some
are out in the open and these
included Conservative Politicians
and Far Right CEO's you see. The
Republican Party has been the
public face of Fascism but so are the
Far Right ultra-nationalistic Think
Tanks pushing American
exceptionalism. The Fascists are
anyone pushing White Identity and
Patriotism. But Fascists come in

many more flavors than I have listed. In Europe, the Fascists are open about their White Supremacism and talk about things like "White Survival". They are openly speaking about a White Identity that must come together to repel the foreign cultural invasion which is supposedly destroying their precious Western culture. Why doesn't anyone talk about a Northern culture. Sweden is 3 hours by flight to the North Pole. Why don't Swedish talk about Northern culture and Northern civilization? When Swedish think of them as Western culture, where are they referencing as the center of the earth for them to be the West? All these fictional and imaginary geographical constructs are nonsense. In America, the Fascists hide as much as they can but in Europe they do not hide. They believe in their exceptionalism and it is this exact mode of thinking that influenced the current Nationalistic White Supremacism practiced by White America (and those that feed at their trough). White America lives in fear of its own shadow. It must be because they fear that minorities and oppressed peoples will figure out that they have been shafted. Screwed over. Used as a Stepping Stone. Does White America fear the 100 million Native Americans that White Americans killed or the 20 million African Americans that White Americans killed? Does White America fear the 5 million or so Muslims that it killed trying to take natural resources like oil and gas? A people that fear their own shadow are a sad lot indeed. Everything a human does in their life has a consequence. Everything a human does has a counter reaction. This is normal, natural, and reasonable. You don't have to have White Guilt but you should feel shame for what America has done if you do consider yourself an American. The Fascists/White Supremacists/Neo-Nazis argue about creating unity among the remnants of Europeans that arrived to the North American continent in order to protect their rights. Protect their rights? White Americans control the Military, White Americans control the Police, White Americans control the Congress, and White Americans control the strings of Business. White Americans should be yelling about protecting everyone else's rights! At least the European Neo-Nazi/White Supremacists admit what they are. Why do the modern Neo-Nazis and White Supremacists in the Republican Party attempt to deny that this is what they are? It has been un-popular since the 1950's to be openly Racist and openly White Supremacist. The White Supremacists went underground but still controlled the strings of power, including the Media (as they do today) and Political Offices. There was no need to be openly Racist anymore when they already practiced Racism through the Institutions under their control. Practicing Racism via institutions (Higher Education, Political Office,

MAKE RACISTS AFRAID AGAIN

Media) was a much more efficient way of ruling over minorities and allowed for there to be a separation in their direct relationship allowing for denial. Coded phrases and terms have replaced the Racism of the past and the new Racist phrases are things like "Build That Wall" and "No More Refugees". When Politicians openly stroke feelings of hatred by scaring the public about one or two or three races, this Hate Speech inadvertently leads to Hate Crimes. The consequences of creating a Hate Culture that excludes certain races and props up other races is that you create an environment that is dictatorial, oppressive, and at its core Racist. Racism cannot be defeated by words alone but it is important to analyze the reason

MAKE RACISTS AFRAID AGAIN

Racism comes about. Increasing gaps in Income Inequality create Racism and Institutions that perpetuate Nationalism (knowing that it leads to Xenophobia) create new Racists. Racism leads to marginalization and it is this that leads to crime, joblessness, and even health related issues.

MAKE RACISTS AFRAID AGAIN

A WEAK UNITY

The unifying factor and the glue that keeps the White Supremacists, Fascists, Neo-Nazis together is their hatred for anyone that is not of them. Their weak and shaky unification revolves around their vile and malice filled hatred for foreigners and foreign nationals, their hatred for Muslims, their hatred for Women, etc. They claim to love humans and not be Neo-Nazis while using logic to justify their reasoning for preventing immigration by refugees. Logical arguments can be used to cover up the reasoning behind Racism but it is does not provide an actual solution for Racism. Logical arguments are made by the Alt-Right to justify their Racism under the guise of things like Patriotism, Nationalism, Safety,

Security, and Well Being. Their arguments are advanced sophist style arguments which are mistaken assumptions knitted together to attempt to convince an un-knowing listener. They are not valid arguments because the assumptions which they are based upon are mistaken. The White Supremacists calls for "White Genocide" are a perfect example of Sophism. The comparison of how many Blacks raped Whites in America versus how many White raped Blacks is using Crime Statistics to project a false image upon an entire people. This is Sophism. It is fallacious and not based on fact. The statistics may be factual but that does not make the argument valid. Since White Americans control the strings of economic power in America, it is they that must protect the minorities and immigrants from the crime that comes with economic hardship. Economic hardship has in the past and does now currently lead to crime. Economic hardship is one of the main factors that leads to Racism especially when the gap between the rich and poor is actually able to be minimized. The progress that is achieved in creating a more equal playing field must be made permanent and pushed socially by educating the public about the hardship experienced by marginalized peoples. Social exclusion and lack of social participation can lead to things like crime as well as leading to health problems among those that are marginalized. Some have argued that marginalization is a result of globalization and the widening gap between the rich and poor. Marginalization is institutional and the policies which can prevent or promote the marginalization of peoples are found within the institutions themselves. The way to deal with the marginalization of people can be done so in a legislative manner as has been witnessed with the "Affirmative Action" policies for organizations. The prevention of marginalization can be done so in a macro manner which would seek to create inclusive environments for politics, economics, and social happenings. A perfect example of marginalization is the way entertainers have been denied credit because of their background. The Father of American Ninjitsu is Professor Ronald Duncan. Ronald Duncan is not credited with being the Father of American Ninjitsu for one reason. Ronald Duncan is Black. As a Black American, his role as the Father of American Ninjitsu was hidden and not discussed in any major Martial Arts magazine. In the 30 plus years I have spent following the Martial Arts, I have rarely heard his name. The name of Ronald Duncan has been neglected and omitted despite Duncan having put on Public Demonstrations of Ninjitsu since the 1960's. In Manhattan in 1968 at the Manhattan Center, various Japanese Masters witnessed Duncan's public exhibition of Ninjitsu. Stephen Hayes, a White male, who is incorrectly credited as the Father of American Ninjitsu, had originally written a letter to Duncan seeking his help to learn Ninjitsu. Duncan gave a referral to Hayes and Hayes went on to Japan and came back in a relatively claiming to be a Ninjitsu Master. Hayes is now invited to events all over the world to lecture as a Ninjitsu Master and Hayes is invited to TedX events to lecture, when it is Professor Duncan that is the Father of American Ninjitsu. Duncan has been bypassed because of his skin color and he has been bypassed because of White Privilege. Similarly, it is Chuck Berry that is the Founder of Rock n Roll but it is Elvis Presley that is incorrectly credited with being the Founder of Rock n Roll.

MAKE RACISTS AFRAID AGAIN

THE LIBERALS IN AMERICA

Liberalism and its left leaning ideals have found popularity and acceptance in greater numbers in urban areas in contrast to rural areas that tend to vote more Conservative. Liberals do tend to be more accepting of new cultures, new ideas, and new ways of thinking. But the Liberals have also been regressive and did not come out in a unified voice during the many military conflicts that started under the Obama administration. It is safe to say that the Anti-War Left was not existent during the 8 years of President Obama. The Liberals have been open critics of the incoming Fascism in America but have also engaged in it when they supported multiple military conflicts overseas

during the Obama administration.
The Liberals have sought to have
their cake and to eat it too. The
Liberals have been weak in their
stance towards the Fascists even
going so far as to accommodate their
desires for deportation. Some of the
Liberals have been vocal and paid lip
service to their disdain for the arrival
of Fascism in America but have not
been willing to make a serious
concerted effort to stop the spread of
it. The inability of Liberals to make a
serious blockade to the racist
policies which have led to things like
Mass Deportations and the Muslim
Travel Ban further demonstrates
their ineptness in the face of
Fascists. The Democratic Party
support the Liberal ideals and
Democratic ideals that unite all races

but have played favorites and allowed certain races to suffer. Nearly 2 million persons were deported under the Obama administration alone. The Liberals have also been un-gracious in their actions towards Anti-Fascists. Liberals have in many cases tried to steal ideas and concepts from the Anti-Fascist Movement without giving credit. The Liberals have been doing this for years. The Liberals in America range from the Moderate Liberals that oppose Abortion to the Berniecrat Liberals that oppose social inequality but support a strong military (war). Many of the Liberals share Fascist ideas but also act as mouthpieces for the Liberal establishment.

MAKE RACISTS AFRAID AGAIN

MDC is an 80's Anti-Fascist Punk Band that inspired much of the Anti-Fascist punk movement. The message of revolt and revolution and anarchy went from the Anti-Fascist Punk Bands of the early 80's in to late 80's Hip Hop. Songs like "Fight the Power" by Public Enemy led Hip Hop in to a direction that was not favored by mainstream music executives. The chant of "No Trump. No KKK. No Fascist USA" used by Green Day at the AMA 2016 awards came from an MDC song "Born to die" with the chant "No War. No KKK. No Fascist USA." The Liberals have tried to brush under and deny the role of the Anti-Fascists in shaping modern Liberal thought. The Liberals have, for the most part, agreed and consented to things like war and military adventurism, which has led to the deaths of hundreds of thousands of lives, if not millions, overseas. There have been several incidents where Anti-Fascists have protested against Far Right groups and Conservative politicians, only to be met with disdain and opposition by Liberals. The recent early 2017 election of Tom Perez to lead the Democratic Party was a clear signal by the Liberal establishment that it did not want a new direction, despite having lost so many Congressional and local seats. Berniecrats or hardcore Bernie Sanders supporters are still acting like they are in a campaign to get Bernie Sanders elected in 2020. They are willing to march in support of Liberal ideals. The problem is that they are not willing to counter-protest or counter-march in to the Fascists to oppose them face to face. The organizers of Liberal marches are more than willing to march away from the Fascists, but unless they agree to march in to the Fascists and deny them the political space, the Fascists will continue growing. The Fascists thrive on a strategy of "March and Grow". Unless the Liberals become willing to march in to Fascists and deny them their opportunity for Hate Speech, the Fascists will continue to do as they have been doing all along. The most famous confrontations between Anti-Fascists and Fascists allowed the Anti-Fascist movement to grow and made the Fascists weaker. Fascists thrive on using force to threaten and achieve dominance. Anti-Fascists have only truly been effective when they have been able to meet the aggression of the Fascists with similar force. It is an unfortunate consequence of the fight against Fascists. Fascists glorify and objectify violence as a way to dominate. Anti-Fascists hate it as much as Liberals do. Liberals have to learn what the Anti-Fascists learned long ago, you have to oppose a Fascist with the same force with which they are bringing down upon you. You want to stand and yell chants in the face of Neo-Nazis and Fascists? If you want to take your nation back from Fascists you have to fight them. If you fail to fight them online and offline, the normalization of hate will become mainstream and it will be too late to oppose them. This conflict has already played out in history many times. In France in the early 80's, you had Neo-Nazis/Fascists beating immigrants to death. They would also beat Black people to death. They (White Supremacists) would beat anyone to death that was not screaming "Rights for Whites". It starts with Hate Speech and ends with Hate Crime. History has on multiple occasions, proven this to be true. You cannot counter Hate Speech with words alone. You have to counter Hate Speech with fists. You have to counter Hate Speech with legislation. You have to counter Hate Speech by the prevention of the gathering of Racists. You have to shut down wherever the Fascists gather. You have to be Pro-Active instead of waiting around like cattle to be hunted. You have to do the hunting online and offline. This is what it is. In early 80's France you had the As-nays (French Black Panthers) with Redskins (Immigrant martial arts masters) and others aligned with them Hunting Neo-Nazis and White Supremacists and Fascists. In England it was Anti-Fascist Action that took on the British National Party and the English Defense League (EDL). In America it is the Antifa (Anti-Fascist) that are opposing the racist and xenophobic policies of the Conservatives and the Republican Party. The Liberals in America have, for the most part, just acted as conduits and apologists for the Fascists by trying to appease them rather than attempting to

67

seriously oppose them. Only by uniting to defeat Fascists in a manner that is pro-active can there be success in the eradication of Hate Speech (which leads to Hate Crime). Reactionary style waiting under the tension created by legitimized Racism cannot stop Fascism. Only pro-active stances and pro-active actions which build a serious barrier to the distribution of hate speech. Hate Speech must be prevented by preventing the Hate Speaker the opportunity to spread their message of Hate. Only by stopping the Hate Speaker, can the Hate Speech be stopped. You cannot Hate Speech by countering it. You have to shut down all Hate Speech by preventing its spread.

MAKE RACISTS AFRAID AGAIN

WHY THEY ARE WINNING

The Fascists are winning in America and will keep winning as long as Liberals keep shunning away from confronting them. Liberals want to take 90 days to organize a Protest and Mobilize to the streets. 90 Days? If Liberals are not able to Mobilize instantly everytime the Fascists march, then the Fascists will keep growing. The Fascists are using the "March and Grow" strategy and are able to Mobilize people on behalf of their cause in short time. The Liberals are wholly ineffective in the face of Fascists. Anti-Fascists view Liberals as being completely comatose in the face of Fascism. Liberals will attend a Trump march and sit in conversation with them while in awe of their lovely Fascist

69

parade. Anti-Fascists get in fist fights everytime they show up at a Fascist march. I have even seen Liberal photographers that I have personally sent to take pictures of Anti-Fascists disrupting a Trump march, coming back with ONLY pictures of Fascists and neglecting the 20 plus Antifa at the march. Liberals are for the most part Cowards that are unable to stand up to Fascists. Liberals are best at bullying each other and oppressing each other while acting like the Fascists will just go away on their own. Fascism is not going away because Fascism feeds off the state (or is it the State feeds off Fascism?). The day that Liberals will be effective is the day that Liberals can Mobilize within one hour to stop Fascists. Liberals want to take 90 days to organize a March when the March has no purpose other than to gather together and chant. The purpose of Mobilization is not chanting and walking in circles. The purpose of Mobilization is to gather up enough persons in a rapid manner that can physically confront (I said confront not fight!!!) Fascists in order to prevent them the physical space and political space to spew their vile Hate Speech. There is no point in Mobilizing if the purpose is not to shut down Fascists.

MAKE RACISTS AFRAID AGAIN

BERNIECRATS

Two words can explain the Berniecrats more than anything else and that is "Flower Power". I get speechless when I think about how inept, weak, and incapable they are in the face of Fascism. Bernie Sanders raised more Defense Industry money in the 2016 Presidential cycle than 10 Republican Candidates combined. If you want to take back your nation, then signing up for a Martial Arts Class will do you more good than will throwing up the peace sign. Bernie Sanders is for a "Strong Military". What do you do with a 600 Billion Dollar a year Defense Budget? You attack nations around the world in order to capture their natural resources and to cause brain drain

72

and capital flight. That is what is done with a "Strong Military". If you are interested in Liberalism, then you would be interested in "No Military". What do you need a Standing Army for? A Standing Army is maintained to invade nations. Since the National Guard already exists, a Standing Army is not only costly but useless unless you plan on using it for military conflict. A true Liberal would say all war is useless when diplomacy exists and with the 30,000 Nuclear weapons American has no nation will be invading any time soon. It is more likely than not that nations around the world are more worried about the vast nuclear arsenals maintained by Western nations than Western nations worried about the latter. Peace is

MAKE RACISTS AFRAID AGAIN

built through diplomacy and interlocking trade networks that allow for the creation of an environment that is conducive to peace-building. If the Berniecrats really believe that they are the actors of the revolution in America that will usher in social harmony, then they must take action to oppose the Fascist directly. Without opposing the Fascists online and offline, the Berniecrats are just preparing a false opposition. Real opposition comes through denying the Fascists the political space online and offline to operate. You cannot stop the Fascists with words alone and you cannot stop the Fascists by shaming them. You can only stop the Fascists by directly opposing them online and offline. When Berniecrats come to this realization, then they will then be able to properly plan what an effective opposition will look like. The Japanese that were placed in internment camps during World War II were done so by a Liberal U.S. President. Do you think that a Conservative U.S. President will be more or less kind to marginalized peoples in the U.S.? We have to build Intersectional Alliances. Anti-Fascists are not of one kind, but of every kind of human imaginable. If we really want to beat the Fascists, we have to invest in the principle of Auto-Defense. In Auto-Defense, we all fight each other's battles. There is no way I have the strength alone to fight all battles (nor do you) but if we all fight the same battle together, then we are all coming to each other's aid. This is the Principle of Auto-Defense. Intersectional Alliances bring the Capability of Auto-Defense. It is us collectively that have to practice the Auto-Defense by coming to each other's aid (whether or not we are effected by the policy we are fighting against).

DIFFERENT APPROACHES

Liberal Approach: Yell and rally about our special interests. Ask the State for help.

Antifa Approach: Lets Physically and Legally Confront and Shut Down Fascists in any form they come in whatever form they come in and then everyone can live in peace.

MAKE RACISTS AFRAID AGAIN

THE BLACK BLOC

The Black Bloc specializes in disruption and fighting. But this name Black Bloc refers to the section of the Antifa just concerned with the three aforementioned items. There are other Special Forces of the Antifa that just hunt Fascists. They hunt Neo-Nazis. Simon Wiesenthal was an Austrian Nazi hunter. Nazis have to be hunted because they are already hunting you and you don't even know about it. Just recently, a video surfaced of a White Nationalist videotaping Indian families playing in a park and ranting about how Indians are stealing tech jobs. Whatever his reason for being angry, including lack of economic prosperity, the fact that you are being hunted is real. First you are caught in their scope and that is what the video was that surfaced. You have to hunt Neo-Nazis/Fascists or they will hunt you. Whether they hunt you with a weapon or whether they hunt you down in a respectable manner using legalized legislation, you are still under their target. Legislation and new laws that hurt your interests are no less harmful to your person than weapons that physically hurt you. This is what it is unfortunately. The sooner you wake up to this reality, the more relieved you will be.

MAKE RACISTS AFRAID AGAIN

OCCUPY MOVEMENT

I read their blogs and they are just as irrelevant today as they were during the Occupy protests. I am sure that the Organizers of the Occupy Movement sleeping in $700 a night Hotel Suites while ordering Don P and Caviar is not in the best interest of the poor. Even today, I read their blogs talking about "Why you should NOT punch Nazis". Why you should not???? How about 100 Reasons Why You Should Punch A Nazi?? Where is your courage in the face of evil? Antifa is not stuck on Punch a Nazi. Physical confrontation is required because Fascists understand this the most. Anti-Fascists may also sue. Anti-Fascists may also Lobby Politicians. Every method is available and will be used.

MAKE RACISTS AFRAID AGAIN

It is not about one method. It is about
multiple methods. Antifa is not "either
or". Anti-Fascists will try all methods.
The major point of all of this is to
create a unified front against the
Fascist so they cannot push their
Hate Speech and normalize it.

DON'T JUSTIFY
RACISM/SEXISM/ETC

The Liberal Media attempts to
explain the Alt-Right in order to
understand it enough to dissect it.
Huffington Post says it's "young
white men who are angry about
income inequality, poor job
prospects, PC culture, crumbling
social welfare programs and war.
They come from Pat Buchanan's
Nativist Paleo-Conservatism, Ron
Paul's Libertarianism, the rape-y

MAKE RACISTS AFRAID AGAIN

Manosphere, the Gamergate underground, and other subcultures". Whatever the reason, you cannot destroy people to destroy ideas. It is like using a sledgehammer to catch a rat hiding in the wall. The best way to stop them is with physical confrontation. Deny them the Political Space to speak their Hate Speech and they will go away. Sue them and weaken them financially. The KKK became irrelevant not because they were lacking in firepower (when they already controlled the Police and the Mayor) but it was by being sued that they had to close up shop. Their Racism never went away and is manifest in the Alt-Right. The Alt-Right's main source for leaks is not surprisingly WikiLeaks. Does that make the information not true? Is it a revelation of any kind that everything you do is watched? If you thought otherwise, then you are living in a false reality. Everything a human does is watched to a certain extent and this is what it has been for 50 years now. Don't promote the Alt-Right's talking points. The Alt-Right In Chief Trump loves it and helps add to the whole bullshit conspiracy world they are living in. By promoting a Culture of Conspiracy, you are engaging in the promotion of Conspiracy. All of these are to sidetrack you from the only goal that is important and that is smashing Fascism. You don't understand how important your role is in a Democracy. Since everyone is equal in a Democracy and you as the Citizen are able to make a

MAKE RACISTS AFRAID AGAIN

Citizen's Arrest, you have the same right as any official. The difference is this. You are not walking around with a gun. It is the gun that enforces the laws of society and keeps order but it is only the Police and their counterparts that have the Legal Authority to use it. This should not stop you from the enforcement of the law because you do not need any weapon to enforce the law. Law enforcement does not require weapons. You as the Citizen of the State are a Law Enforcer. The Democratic model requires you to think of yourself as more than a consumer. The Democratic model requires you to think of yourself as the enforcer of laws with the vigilance that is required to prevent things social injustice. In a

MAKE RACISTS AFRAID AGAIN

Democracy, the Citizen is the enforcement and the representative for justice. The Police cannot and will not always be there and if they are, this does not guarantee that justice will be carried out. If you wait for people to intervene on your behalf, you will be waiting forever because no one can save you but yourself. In order to bring justice, you have to own justice and carry justice in your own hands. This is the role of the Citizen in a Democracy. To hold the local officials accountable, hold the Politicians accountable, and to hold other Citizens and residents accountable.

MAKE RACISTS AFRAID AGAIN

THE CONSERVATIVES IN AMERICA

America is in a serious denial about what it has become. Imagine, if you heard of some nation on the other side of the globe and they told you that this nation has been at war for the past 224 of the last 240 years. Would you conclude that this nation is a peaceful nation or would you come to the conclusion that this nation is dangerous? For years, the majority White Americans made decisions as if minorities did not exist. Grievances were not met and problems were left unsolved. Racist language used by the Status Quo in America was tempered and minorities were quick to stay silent in the face of Racism in order to prevent conflict from occurring. In

MAKE RACISTS AFRAID AGAIN

America, if you are a White
American you are considered a
"Real American" and are just
referred to as an American. If a
minority is spoken of in America,
then the media will refer to them as
African-American or Latin American
or Mexican American. This openly
implies that minority are treated as
2nd class citizens and are not equal
in the receiving of the benefits and
privileges as White America. This is
why Racism is Institutional, because
the practices of the institutions are
the ones that implement the racist
policies that marginalize minorities.
The Conservatives in America and
the individuals that associate with
their Far Right teachings have
openly promoted racism, bigotry,
xenophobia, sexism, transphobia,

speciesism, nationalism, pro-
militarism, hatred for foreigners, and
supremacism. They have spoken of
creating an Ethno-State which seeks
to only bring in immigrants that will
assimilate and will drive out
immigrants that are troublesome.
The Conservatives embrace and
glorify militarism and nationalism and
this was clearly evident in Trump's
early 2017 1st Speech to Congress.
The use of political propaganda to
sell endless war and to dehumanize
the victims of endless war while
victimizing invading soldiers, is a key
tool of the Fascists. The victims of
aggression are never remembered
or mentioned, but they are
dehumanized and made to be less
than human. The soldiers that are
killed fighting overseas are made to

be as heroes fighting for an ideal
known as freedom. Did the people
within the nations being invaded feel
like they were being given freedom
or did they feel they were being
invaded by a foreign hostile force?
To continue selling an endless war
you have to create visible symbols
that can be both victims and heroes.
The Far Right is united under two
things mostly, Racist hate of others
and Supremacism. Trump
Republicans are a unique breed of
Fascists unto themselves, with their
own unique terminology. Wildly
outrageous conspiracy theories like
Pizzagate are talked about openly as
are a "Socialist Takeover" of the
United States. Just judging from a
recent Trump Republican rally in
Arizona that featured State officials

in attendance, it seemed more like a gathering of conspiracy theorists and White Supremacists. Even some of the minorities that attended were echoing the same mantra and terminology used by the Alt-Right and White Supremacists in America. A 13-year-old boy whom supported Trump who gave an interview to a local news network said something like "That Jew over there better keep her mouth shut" while pointing to a person he had previously argued with. The feeling of open Anti-Semitism and Xenophobia (hatred of foreigners and foreign nationals) was straight out of a Hitler Youth rally. The cult-like demeanor of many of the attendees and their blind obedience to anything Trump, would make exchanging with them in

MAKE RACISTS AFRAID AGAIN

logical debate a difficult one for
anyone that disagreed. The feeling
more than anything was an exclusive
one. The environment excluded
anyone that seemingly did not agree
with building a wall, deporting
immigrants, or turning away refugees
from the Syrian conflict. The uniting
factor among the attendees was
above all their hatred for anything
that seemed foreign and their love
for anything even remotely
American. The Alt-Lite is the lighter
version of the Alt-Right which moves
between the Conservative and the
Alt-Right ideology. The Alt-Right
ideology is about White Identity and
White Survival. The Alt-Lite wants
the best of both worlds, Conservative
Libertarian ideology with White
Identity. Richard Spencer is most

MAKE RACISTS AFRAID AGAIN

certainly the High Priest of the Alt-
Right (along with White Supremacist
David Duke) and Alex Jones and
Paul Joseph Watson of InfoWars
have been the mouth pieces for the
Alt-Lite. Alex Jones and PJ Watson
still sell White Supremacism
(knowingly or unknowingly) by
openly engaging in the ridiculing of
Black Lives Matter, Muslims, and
calling for an end to the entry of
refugees. The Conservatives are not
liked by Richard Spencer's Alt-Right
or David Duke's White Supremacists.
The Conservatives (Republican
Party) are referred to as
Cuckservatives. This is what they
are called by the Alt-Right. David
Duke's Alt-Right views the
Republican Party aka Conservatives
differently in that he views most of

91

them as having sold out the White race. In other words, David Duke views many Conservatives as being traitors to the White race. Trump was able to satisfy many people in the Alt-Right and within White Supremacists with his Anti-Immigration policies which have led to a general feeling of Islamophobia and Xenophobia in the United States. In early 2017, Richard Spencer was asked to leave the CPAC conference of Conservatives (which Trump also intended), because his views were seen as being too extreme. But is highly unlikely that was the genuine reason that Spencer was thrown out. It is more than likely that Spencer was thrown out because Spencer's Alt-Right ideology posed a threat to the

MAKE RACISTS AFRAID AGAIN

mainstream Conservative ideology
which the CPAC conference was
presenting. Also, it did not hurt for
the mainstream Conservatives to
make a public display of distancing
themselves politically and
ideologically from Spencer, was now
taking the political heat in the
mainstream media for his views.
Richard Spencer's Alt-Right is just
more of the same Fascism that has
presented itself throughout history.
The playbook is old and the plays
are even older. It starts with creating
a unique identity (White Identity or
America First!!) as a unifying call for
gathering, then immigrants are
scapegoated, people with different
religions are scapegoated and
attacked, the Freedom of the Press
is diminished and called Fake News,

MAKE RACISTS AFRAID AGAIN

labor unions are seen as enemies of business, military/police/security presence is increased, art education budgets are cut while militarism is promoted, the media begins to normalize the Fascism to protect its ability to make money while slightly verbally attacking it, politicians begin to appease the Fascism rather than to remove it, and people in power begin to openly discuss things like creating an Ethno-State. Many of the views of Trump are directly from the Alt-Right. The notion of creating an Ethno-State is not new. 100 million Native Americans and 20 million African Americans were murdered by White Americans in order to create the majority White America that exists today. Immigration officials gave preference to Europeans in

order to maintain the correct racial
make up that would allow White
Americans to maintain majority rule.
The Alt-Lite is much more advanced
in pushing White Supremacism
because it does so under the cover
of Conservative Libertarianism. They
even go so far as to refer to
themselves as Classical Liberals,
that are fighting off a Leviathan type
Government that wants to take away
your rights (and in their view your
guns). Nationalism is packaged and
sold as the answer to problems (a
typical Fascist view) and Immigrants
are scapegoated as the force behind
all problems of society. The Alt-Lite
(which Trump subscribes to) and the
Alt-Right are currently in a battle for
supremacy (White Supremacists
fighting over who has the better

viewpoint). The current Republican Party conservatives have tried to distance themselves from the Alt-Right in order to create a political barrier while echoing the talking points of the Alt-Right. Whether they call themselves the Alt-Lite or Alt-Right, they both share the same racist, xenophobic, nationalistic, anti-immigrant attitudes. The Alt-Right has started multiple channels on YouTube for defeating Anti-Fascists (Antifa). The channels are based around following around Anti-Fascists and showing them in a negative light. Unfortunately for the Alt-Right and the Conservatives, the channels have only helped Antifa gain international exposure resulting in its rapid growth. It is a long term project by the Alt-Right to shame and

MAKE RACISTS AFRAID AGAIN

disgrace the only opposition to
Fascism in America. Leaders of local
Republican Party clubs in California
(as well as other states) spend their
time online trolling Anti-Fascists. It is
a waste of time for them because
they are automatically blocked as a
security precaution to prevent them
from sharing their Hate Speech in
public. They (local Republican
leaders in California) have gone as
far as to create videos on YouTube
that try to show them as not being
Neo-Nazis. You don't have to be a
Neo-Nazi to be a Fascist but you are
indeed a Fascist if you are a Neo-
Nazi. You are a Fascist if you are
selling Patriotism and/or Nationalism
because this leads to Xenophobia.
There is nothing wrong with having
feelings of love and admiration for

your nation. The evil is in hiding
Racism within this love and
admiration. The social media
channels that the Alt-Right have
launched to directly attack Anti-
Fascists are used to supposedly
expose Anti-Fascists and to shame
them. Shame them? There are 95
million people unemployed in 2017.
What is more shameful than this for
a nation that claims to be First
World? The Republicans and
Democrats that have led America in
to an endless cycle of war that has
bankrupted the nation, are the ones
that should be in shame! There is no
shame to feel when you are not
accepted in to society. Only when
you are given employment, given
social standing, and given
acceptance, can you feel shame.

MAKE RACISTS AFRAID AGAIN

Until then, it is the White Supremacist loving establishment that should feel shame for robbing the people of the American Dream! White Supremacists use The Crusades as their rallying point to express how the current refugees and immigrants entering the United States are just a Muslim invasion. I cannot for the life of me figure out how refugees escaping from a War Zone can be compared to a Christian invasion of the Middle East. How are these two compared logically? Did the Middle Easterners themselves create 65 million refugees in their own neighborhoods in order to lose all their belongings and flee for their lives? How does England, which at one point in history held 100 colonies, complain about

MAKE RACISTS AFRAID AGAIN

immigrants? How does France, which invaded, raped, and pillaged so many African nations, complain about African immigrants? How does that work? The 1st Crusade by Christians was a motley crew of thieves, rapists, murderers, killers, a few Religious pilgrims, and vagabonds that killed and raped their way across Europe. The 2nd Crusade was also similar. The religious fervor experienced by Christians during the Crusades is very comparable to the extremist hate filled (fundamentalist Sunni Islam) ISIS ideology. White Supremacists and Neo-Nazis have vandalized mosques in places like Glasgow, Scotland with the Crusader era words "Deus Volt" written on walls. Mosques have been vandalized in multiple places in the United States in places like Hawaii, the Midwest, and in California. The rallying cry and talk in 2017 about the Crusades is a Racist coded reminder that America is a Christian nation that must stop the out of control horde of Muslims entering. The Muslim Travel Ban that was pushed by Trump was an example of scapegoating a people in order to gain political points with followers as well as to send a warning message to Muslim-Americans. Thankfully, the Muslim Travel Ban was frozen by two separate Judges because it is un-Constitutional. But that did not prevent the public outcry that came with it. Tens of thousands of persons around the U.S. protested at Airports and local and national Politicians

used their clout to free the travelers
stuck in limbo. In the end, the Muslim
Travel Ban failed but was a clear
sign and foreshadowing of the
attitudes maintained by many in the
United States towards marginalized
peoples like Muslim-Americans. The
Democratic Party leaders played a
role in awakening discontent via
media so that people became aware
of the Muslim Travel Ban and the
Republican Party as well as the Alt-
Right cheered on its arrival. The
Racists really came out completely
un-afraid once they had received
validation for their beliefs by Trump
by his Muslim Travel Ban. The
promotion of the Muslim Travel Ban
by Trump and its initial engineering
by Rudy Guliani, was celebrated by
White Supremacists in the United

MAKE RACISTS AFRAID AGAIN

States as a victory for the protection of White Identity. By excluding one or two or three or more races, the American Government itself had now become a unified institution for the promotion of Racism. Whether intentional or not, this is what the Muslim Travel Ban was in essence stating to the world. That a nation of immigrants only accepted certain types of immigrants with only specific religions. The illegal Muslim Travel Ban was not only deeply embarrassing for the United States but it was greatly revealing as to the extent that White Nationalism and White Supremacist thought dominates American political thought. It was the arrival of immigrants to the New World that made America a melting pot and it is

MAKE RACISTS AFRAID AGAIN

the settling of new immigrants in to
America that will allow it to progress.
When Racism becomes normalized,
the individuals living in the society,
whether in the Status Quo, Middle
Class, or Working Class, are
affected by its effects. Everyone
begins to think of anyone but
themselves as being un-safe.
Everyone grows suspicious of
anyone that is not like them. Racism
breeds public suspicion and it leads
to shunning and marginalizing
individuals. When people become
marginalized, they are unable to take
part in and to enjoy the benefits of
living in that society. They are unable
to get married, unable to find a job,
unable to find anyone to have a child
with, unable to make friends, and
unable to adjust/settle in to society.

MAKE RACISTS AFRAID AGAIN

Marginalized peoples like Muslim-Americans that are openly treated like 2nd class citizens cannot adjust to openly racist conditions except by retreating further in to their own communities. How can you expect a marginalized person to feel comfortable in a society that has relegated them to a 2nd class citizen? Only when marginalized peoples enjoy the same benefits and privileges as everyone else can they be expected to be normal functioning members of society. Until then, it is safe to assume that by marginalizing individuals the State is engaging in State Sponsored Oppression. What about Liberal states like California? Do Muslim-Americans fare any better? No. Liberals are no less bigoted within their hearts against

MAKE RACISTS AFRAID AGAIN

Muslim-Americans than
Conservatives are, it is just that the
Conservatives are foolish enough to
mouth their Racism and to try to
legalize it via legislation. The
Liberals harbor the same hatred and
Racism against Muslims that the
Conservatives have and many of the
Liberals I personally know in Los
Angeles did not protest against the
racist bigoted Muslim Travel Ban
because of this. Just because
someone has Liberal values does
not mean that they are not a Fascist
just as someone having
Conservative values does not
automatically make them a Fascist. It
is what they say and do that makes
them a Fascist. A perfect example of
a Fascist is Milo Yiannopolous. Milo
is hailed as the mouthpiece of the

MAKE RACISTS AFRAID AGAIN

Alt-Lite and spends his time verbally attacking immigrants, refugees, Feminists, Muslims, and anyone that disagrees with the Alt-Lite ideology. Milo's speaking tours have been the center of controversy and he has enjoyed the benefits of the attention through via earned media. Milo's focus on verbally attacking Muslims in the name of Nationalism and protecting Western (White Identity) culture is the very meaning of Fascism. His appeal to Conservatives that are also Feminists (started by White women) has been growing steadily through his tours. He attempts to bypass and to sweep under the rug the amount of Racism and Bigotry faced by marginalized peoples in the U.S. By doing so, he only increases the amount of individuals that will seek not to assimilate but will further associate only with their own community out of a need for safety and self-preservation. You cannot sell the inclusiveness and melting pot nature of America by excluding certain individuals because of their beliefs. One of the major signs of Fascism is indeed scapegoating. Creating false where none exist in order to establish law and order is another clear sign of Fascism. Social exclusion has long term effects for the community and Hate Speakers like Milo feel no remorse when stoking the flames of hate simply because Milo does not and has not permanently resided in the United States. No American that loves their nation would practice bigotry, social exclusion, marginalization, and oppression in order to sell more books.

PLAYING THEM OFF

Are male and female immigrants in the United States treated the same? No. Female immigrants are greeted with open arms in many cases while male immigrants take most of the oppression. Why is this? Because female immigrants are viewed as more stable in income production and are possible sources of child birth. Immigrant men may have no job or be forced to do odd jobs while immigrant women may be given better positions or positions of responsibility. Male immigrants have it much more difficult and face not only the discrimination and loathing that comes with being an immigrant, but are also viewed with suspicion as in the case of Muslim-Americans. Female immigrants that immigrated from Muslim nations are not viewed with the same suspicion and loathing as male immigrants that immigrated from Muslim nations. Male immigrants are then less vocal in their opposition to policies that persecute and marginalize them while female immigrants have an almost protected status when voicing their displeasure over political policies. In contrast to female immigrants, male immigrants are more likely than not to face Racism without responding to it for the sake of maintaining their status in society. This creates a situation where Racism is acknowledged but not dealt with for the sake of procuring one's next meal. It is a vicious cycle that is institutional (because female immigrants are given visas easier) and will continue to affect newly arriving immigrants as long as its practice continues. All immigrants should be treated equally to citizens so that the nation can attempt to achieve some form of national unity and harmony.

It has not been surprising that the growth of Fascism in America has fueled anti-immigration rhetoric among minorities. Many minorities including Mexican-Americans, African-Americans, and Asian Americans have embraced Fascism to the detriment of their own people. Why would minorities be affected by

MAKE RACISTS AFRAID AGAIN

Pro-Nationalism and Anti-Immigration views by the government? America has a long running myth of "superiority" that it sells to the world through movies, music, books, and news. Minorities are not affected any less than the Status Quo when confronted with this myth of superiority. Minorities from a specific nation that arrived in America earlier than other immigrants, will view incoming immigrants from that same nation as being less than American. Minorities that have been in America for long periods of time, like African American or Blacks, have been openly Racist and Bigoted towards Africans coming in to America. Africans coming to America face a distinct and very targeted racism that

MAKE RACISTS AFRAID AGAIN

just focuses on making Africans feel
not welcome. I have been told
personally been told on multiple
occasions by Africans that had
moved to America, that they were
facing deep levels of Racism from
Black Americans, resulting in them
being shunned and marginalized in
society. Minorities are not racist, but
by the Status Quo pushing Anti-
Immigration propaganda and
promoting the Myth Of Superiority,
this has led to many individuals
among minorities, becoming openly
racist and openly bigoted. In 2017
America, it is not uncommon to see a
Mexican-American woman yelling
and complaining about immigration
from Mexico. This is because this
person and other persons are
affected by the Myth of Superiority

which America sells to the world. The person that arrived in America before the newly arrived immigrant, view themselves as being more American and newly arriving immigrants as being not American or less American. If Racism against Immigrants is growing among minorities, it is because many people are being conditioned by mantras like "America First" to dislike or hate immigrants. Immigrants to the United States are no less American than any other immigrant to the United States. Since the only people that can claim to be American are Native Americans, then everyone else that has arrived on the North American continent since 1492 is just another immigrant. Old immigrants should not judge new immigrants. We are all immigrants.

THIRTY THINGS YOU CAN DO

What are some things that you can do to Make Racists Afraid Again?

1. Stop supporting Movies and TV shows that sell Racist viewpoints and that scapegoat peoples

2. Don't Engage in Hate Speech

3. If you see someone talking Hate Speech, ask them to Stop.

4. Don't make jokes about people's religion, race, nationality, beliefs, gender, etc.

5. Don't support Patriotic views knowing that it creates an environment that is exclusive.

6. Don't yell about the evils of Globalism while enjoying the fruits (products) of its labor.

7. Don't talk about how great Nationalism is when you know that Nationalism caused 200 million deaths in the 20th century (World War I and World War II).

8. If you see a Hate Sticker or Hate Flyer on a bulletin board, then remove it and throw it in the trash.

9. Ask people in your neighborhood to form an Anti-Racism Neighborhood Watch to protect each other.

10. Document (take pictures) hate crimes and report them to local authorities so that they are aware of the growing problem in their area.

11. Use Social Media to fight Racism. Post Anti-Racist memes that seek to unite all peoples regardless of their background.

12. Contact local Politicians and ask them to attend an Anti-Racism march in your area.

MAKE RACISTS AFRAID AGAIN

13. Organize an Anti-Racism March to unite people of all backgrounds against bigotry.

14. Contact the landlord where a Hate Group is renting office space and inform the landlord of the Hate Group's activities.

15. Contact the School Board if you find out a Teacher in your area is teaching Hate Speech against marginalized peoples.

16. Spend one day a week volunteering for an organization or group that is working for immigrants' rights.

17. Organize a Clean Up crew and paint over Racist insignias and graffiti.

18. Spend one day a week calling organizations from various backgrounds in order to form a broad coalition against Racism.

19. Host an Art Show that features Art with Anti-Racist messages.

20. Boycott companies that engage in Racist policies.

21. If you see something Racist, then say something about it and be vocal. Silence is the same as consent.

22. Don't think your Race is superior to anybody else's. No Race on earth is better or more important than any other Race. If you want to defeat Racists, then you have to first defeat the Racist within your own being.

23. Don't act in an ethno-centric manner and think that your nationality is better than anybody else on earth. There are over 200 nations on earth and all of them are worth of respect and admiration.

24. Don't play favorites. Respect all people equally unless they have disrespected you in a

manner that deserves mutual reciprocation.

25. Attempt to learn about other cultures by reading about them and engaging them in conversation.

26. Learn a 2nd language or better yet a 3rd language. The more languages you speak the more in-depth understanding you will have of different cultures.

27. Avoid engaging in Superiority debates. Superiority debates are useless and Racist at their core. Shun Superiority debates.

28. Listen to viewpoints of people you disagree with and attempt to understand them.

29. Travel the world. This is the fastest way to change your view on foreign cultures.

30. Have Compassion. Racists are racist because they lack compassion. Humans with compassion love other humans.

MAKE RACISTS AFRAID AGAIN

THIRD WAVE FEMINISM

The Feminist movement was based around the need to establish Voting Rights (Suffrage) for women. Women were not able to vote in elections and this made them marginalized and oppressed in American society. More than one hundred and fifty rallies and protests were held by Feminists until American women gained the right to vote. Modem Feminism (3rd wave Feminism) current fight is for women to have Equal Pay in the workplace, meaning their salaries or working hours granted should be no less than a man. Women do deserve Equal Pay in the workplace and the Feminists have an uphill battle in making this a reality. There should be as many female CEO's of Fortune

MAKE RACISTS AFRAID AGAIN

500 companies as there are male CEO's. Modern Feminism is a White Female's franchise and it was not un-common to hear African-American women and Latin women of complaining about the lack of inclusion contained within the Women's March movement. Just based on research on social media blogs and sites by Feminists and Feminist groups, it is easy to spot how Muslim American women, Black women, and Mexican-American women are treated with neglect and made to feel invisible. This is because Feminism is a movement that grew out of privileged White American women's groups. There were many Feminists that were poor and even Middle Class that participated in marches in the early

MAKE RACISTS AFRAID AGAIN

20th century, but it is the Rich that have the ability to "make noise" without facing backlash because of it. Thus it was the rich Feminists of the early 20th Century that funded Feminism as a movement and as an ideology, despite the masses of the women (poor and middle class) using it to gain power. As a White women's movement, Feminism is exclusive which means that it is not inclusive. Rarely are Women of color made heroines other than to show the world how "Liberal" we all can be.

MAKE RACISTS AFRAID AGAIN

SHOULD YOU TALK TO FASCISTS?

Dialogue is good and can help to prevent mis-communication. Los Angeles is a multi-cultural city and will never be an "Ethno-State" like what many Trump supporters wish to usher in. Fascism comes in many forms and flavors, but all of the Fascist movements share one thing in common, their love for their nation and their hate for foreign nationals. Nationalism, as any student of history can show you, has led to things like Xenophobia (hate of foreign nationals). Anti-Fascists are standing against the Fascist attitudes which are dangerously shaping America. Anti-Fascists do not mean harm to anyone whatsoever but Anti-Fascists cannot stand by idly while

126

MAKE RACISTS AFRAID AGAIN

America transforms in to a Fascist
state. Europe has already
experienced what America is
experiencing and so has England.
Let us ask victims of the National
Front and British National Party if
yelling "Rights for Whites" made
England more united or more
divided. Racism has never been a
strong unifier. The alliance shared by
Racists and Fascists is shaky at best
because its essence is rooted in
hatred and a lack of understanding.
The hatred of foreign nationals by
the Far Right is firmly rooted in
hatred and lack of understanding.
The "He Will Not Divide Us" Flag of
celebrity Shia Lebeouf that was
recently hoisted in Liverpool,
England in an Arts Center, was
ripped down by Fascist online and

MAKE RACISTS AFRAID AGAIN

offline troll groups (4Chan and 8Chan). 4Chan works in the media sector and 8Chan does disruption operations on Liberals. 8Chan ripped down the Flag that was on top of the 5th story roof of the Arts Center building and the Flag pole was over 5 meters tall. 8Chan made their way via rooftop of another building and were able to take down the Flag resulting in the cancellation of Shia Lebeouf's 4-year Live Stream Protest. This is just another example of the extent the Fascists will go to in order to shut down the "Freedom of Speech" they love so dearly. Fascists will go to even greater attempts to shut down the Freedom of Speech and that is because they do not want dissenting opinions to create problems for the messages they have previously presented to society. If Fascists claim to love the Freedom of Speech so greatly, why is it that they have problems with protestors that exercise their Freedom of Speech to dissent against them? Is Freedom of Speech only available to the Fascists but not available for the Protestors that dissent against their messages?

MARCH 25 2017 - LA

"100 Trump supporters which included White Supremacists, Anti-Immigration advocates, Anti-Islam hate speakers, and general bigots, gathered at the Trump Star on Hollywood Blvd to support Trump. Approximately 20 Anti-Fascists (in total) protested against Trump and 3 Anti-Fascists were arrested and/or

taken in to custody by Police. The
names of the 3 Anti-Fascists
arrested have not been identified but
Anti-Fascists in Los Angeles are
working to secure their release and
to gather funding for their bail.
Despite being outnumbered and
surrounded, the 20 Anti-Fascists
protested against Trump in the noisy
and chaotic environment of
Hollywood Blvd, while under the
constant surveillance of law
enforcement. Los Angelesians
showed extreme apathy in allowing
Fascists (Trump supporters) to
openly parade through Hollywood.
But their Fascism did not go un-
contested as masked Anti-Fascists
made their presence felt. More time
spent organizing will yield a greater
volume of individuals to protest

against Fascism. In Huntington Beach, there were Trump supporters carrying the Nazi Iron Cross Flag in the Trump March. As this fact has been documented in picture form and by multiple witnesses, this fact is indisputable and beyond disputation of any kind. Anti-Semitic remarks were openly uttered by Trump supporters in the Trump March that occurred on March 25th, 2017 in Huntington Beach. Police dogs attacked at least one Anti-Fascist that was protesting against the openly bigoted policies of Trump. Chants like "Build that Wall" are openly racist but some of the older Trump supporters are much more sophisticated preferring a muted Racism which expresses itself through Patriotism. Two African-

131

MAKE RACISTS AFRAID AGAIN

American Anti-Fascists that were in
Huntington Beach on March 25th,
2017 to protest against Trump were
attacked by Neo-Nazis. Nazi era
Flags were used in the march and
openly racist comments were hurled
at Anti-Trump protestors. There was
a group there called Defend America
that was an openly Fascist group
and they were chanting Fascist
slogans like "You can't run, you can't
hide, you get a helicopter ride". This
slogan was alluding to the favorite
Fascist/Neo-Fascist method of
disposing of opponents which is
throwing them out of a helicopter.
The two African-American Anti-
Fascists were jumped by a group of
10 or 12 Trump people and at least
one of them was hit in the face with
Brass Knuckles by Trump

MAKE RACISTS AFRAID AGAIN

supporters. A reporter for the OC
Weekly newspaper in Orange
County was called Fake News,
assaulted and punched by Trump
supporters. Neo-Nazis openly
paraded and the Trump march
organizers made no effort to remove
them from the march. Police made
no attempt to arrest the Trump
supporters that assaulted the OC
Weekly reporter. Police only arrested
Anti-Trump protestors. Police
attempted to pacify and calm down
Trump supporters who were worked
up in to a patriotic fervor from
chanting nationalistic mantras. The
September 11 remembrance Day is
Racist to the hilt. This day conjures
up feelings of Islamophobia. Only 1
nation out of the 40 Muslim nations
was involved in the terrorist attack on

133

the Twin Towers in New York City. Yet 9/11 has become a Rallying Cry to justify Islamophobia while screaming for greater security. The loss of Civil Rights and the slippery slope towards Fascism began in America with the event known as September 11. After this event, Americans lost greater freedom and it was justified for security. Benjamin Franklin said "He who would give up liberty for a little security, deserves neither." Trump supporters, who pride themselves on being so freedom loving, have had no qualms or misgivings about giving up their freedom to gain greater security, to their own detriment. Muslims are scapegoated as the danger to America, when it is in fact the White Supremacists that are armed with

machine guns and it is the White
Supremacists that are forming in to
militias with high powered weapons.
Muslim Americans are scared of
their own shadow for fear of being
blamed for anything. Americans
should be scared of White
Supremacists because they
practically worship gun culture and
they more than likely own more than
one firearm. Using scapegoats to
blame the problems of society on
only creates greater between varying
peoples living within the same
society. Unity has never been
achieved by scapegoating a people.

MAKE RACISTS AFRAID AGAIN

DO YOU THINK THEY ARE QUITTING?

The White Americans killed 100 million Native Americans. You might think this is just a historical fact to think about but history is one long sequence of events. This is why individuals and organizations view the track records or histories of other individuals or organizations. To understand what someone will do, all you have to do is look at their past. Humans run on patterns and this is because behavior is automated. Because behavior is automated, behavior is predictable. If America has spent the last 224 years out of the past 240 years at war, what do you think the next 240 years will look like? Probably more of the same. Behavior is automated and runs in patterns. Fascists are supporting the use of Police to beat down activists and Fascists are celebrating ganging up on protestors in marches. Conservative talk show host and Vice co-founder Gavin McInnis celebrates punching protestors. Protestors are protesting because they feel they're so fed up and angered by an issue that they are publicly voicing their opinions out of a need for social justice. Fascists are the ones that attempt at every turn to shut down activists and protestors. Fascists are the ones that call everything they do not agree with Fake News. The Far Right extremists, Fascists, White Supremacists, and Neo-Nazis have little or zero Journalistic Integrity. They spend their time online attacking media outlets that they believe are ruining their domination over the facts. The Far Right are invested in Alternative Facts. CNN and the Washington Post was unable to get Hillary Clinton elected because it is the Far Right media that are dominating in the United States. Hillary Clinton was 100 percent correct about there being a Vast Right Wing Conspiracy in the United States.

MAKE RACISTS AFRAID AGAIN

CAN TECH STOP RACISM?

When all the services available to a
resident, visa applicant, or citizen are
automated and electronic, it is safe
to assume that there will be a more
even accommodation in the
fulfillment of services rendered by
local, State, and Federal
Government. The question remains
however if indeed technology can
erase Racism. Computers can be
just as Racist or more Racist than
humans, if their decision making
process is shaped by individuals with
a White Supremacist or even Ethno-
Nationalist agenda. Technology can
provide an even playing field in the
registering, allocation, and
distribution of things like Government
services. E-Government can play a
huge role in automating routine

procedures thereby preventing bureaucrats the ability to pre-judge an individual based on their ethnicity, race, religion, etc. Names reveal more than we admit and there have been countless cases of Americans being denied services because of their name sounding "too ethnic" or sounding foreign. Immigrants, in many areas of the United States, face an uphill battle when dealing with local and State officials. The automation of routine processes like filing for permits and other key governmental services can prevent individuals from denying people services because of their background. But automation implies the reverse engineering and re-creation of a process with the aim of optimizing by automating it using software. If the process design is flawed and builds in Racism in to it, then the Computer might become the main oppressor of humans, without the guilt or remorse that humans would feel. Humans could trust in computers to carry out Racist policies while having no moral dilemma about it because the computer is the one doing the oppression, not the human. Ultimately, it is the human that defines the experience for other humans in software creation. Racism can be reduced or minimized by creating an even playing field for Electronic Government (E-Government) services, but the humans that design the software must be willing to omit parameters that exercise racist policies. Racism cannot be totally eradicated using digital systems but at least it can be reduced and mitigated and weakened. Automation in service allocation allows for an equal and anti-racist method of providing key services for individuals and organizations. As the move towards E-Government becomes a reality, there will be a greater trend towards achieving social equality regarding services that are allocated to residents of a community by their respective government.

MAKE RACISTS AFRAID AGAIN

WHAT CAN YOU DO?

You can begin by doing Anti-Racist activities.

1. Anti-Racist activities - Patrolling areas for Racist stickers and racist propaganda (wall flyers, etc.).

a. Taking a picture of them

b. Ripping them down

c. Putting an Antifa sticker over it (or a Hello Kitty sticker if you are all out of Antifa stickers)

d. Documenting the location

e. Entering the location in to a Map so you can find patterns in Racist activity

RACIST BEAUTY

The concept of beauty is a conditioned behavior and thus how we view beauty is largely a fictional construct that has been programmed in to our psyche from childhood. I was recently watching an episode of Black Talk Show host Tommy Sotomayor (who only or mostly dates White women) in which he stated "Without White women, Black people don't exist or are not pretty" and that "You have to mix Black blood with White people or else they will not look good". Let us forget how deeply Racist and child-like these two statements are and just focus on the facts. Since the concept of beauty and what is or is not beautiful has been programmed in to us since childhood, it is a conditioned behavior. Who can decide what is beautiful and what is not beautiful. Beauty, as the saying goes, is in the eyes of the beholder. It is Racist, Supremacist, and Fascist to say that Black people are not pretty if they are not mixed. It is Racist and Supremacist for Tommy Sotomayor to say that "Black women feature at the bottom of the pick on dating sites". Black women are no less attractive to a White man than a White woman is. Beauty is naturally defined by certain things in women including having a long neck, being tall, the woman having the majority of her body weight in her hips, large breasts, etc. It is inconceivable to think that a White man is not attracted to a Black woman the same way he will be to a White woman.

145

MAKE RACISTS AFRAID AGAIN

Excessive melanin or lack of
melanin, will not dictate
attractiveness and beauty, but the
White Supremacist and American-
centric beauty magazines in New
York have engaged in the practice of
promoting White women as the
standard of beauty, to the detriment
of Brown and Black women. It is
more than likely that our concept of
beauty was shaped at a very early
age and that it was based on the
faces we saw in childhood. Tommy
Sotomayor is using his past negative
experiences with Black women and
projecting that to an entire race while
using racist generalizations (they are
always angry, etc.) to justify why he
only or mostly dates White women.
His concept of beauty is White
Supremacist and American-centric

but his expressions of his views on the matter range from logical to downright malicious and hurtful. Beauty is not based on colors; beauty is based on attraction. Attraction is not based on melanin, but is based on natural physical features that have existed for tens of thousands of years in the modern human. Beauty and attraction depends on various elements that just cannot be summed up with attributing them to physical features alone. Beauty and attraction are conditioned behaviors but their essence remains as of yet undefined.

MAKE RACISTS AFRAID AGAIN

ZIONISM & ANTI-SEMITISM

How does both Zionism and Anti-Semitism exist in the Far Right in American politics? How can they both thrive and survive in the Right Wing? The Alt-Right and the White Supremacists have been openly Anti-Semitic. The result? Just in the first three months of 2017, there were nearly one hundred threats to Jewish Community Centers and Synagogues. America's relationship with Israel has been vastly tightened in the first three months of 2017 as well. It is undeniable that both increasing ties with Israel and threats to Jewish people are coming from the Right Wing in America. Has the recent surge of Fascism in America (Pro-Nationalism and Anti-Immigration) fueled Anti-Semitism?

MAKE RACISTS AFRAID AGAIN

Without a doubt. Jewish people are viewed by many in the Right Wing as being part of a financial conspiracy to control the United States. The Far Right and/or White Supremacists also view Jewish people as not being White. In other words, Jewish people are viewed by White Supremacists as being foreigners in the United States. Synagogues have been vandalized and in the Mid-west have even been shot at in the first three months of 2017. Benjamin Netanyahu, who is the Prime Minister of Israel, went so far as to commend Trump for taking the initiative to create a border Wall between Mexico and the United States. Right Wing politicians tend to agree with each other, if not work together. The rise of Anti-Semitism

MAKE RACISTS AFRAID AGAIN

has been fueled by racist and bigoted Internet memes coming from the Far Right. The growth of Neo-Nazi groups that meet online has allowed White Supremacists to organize and promote their Anti-Semitic activities. The greater the Anti-Immigration and Pro-Nationalism fervor is increased in America, the greater will be the Hate Crimes aimed at Jewish people.

MAKE RACISTS AFRAID AGAIN

30 ANTI-FASCIST CHANTS

1. No Trump, No KKK, No fascist USA

2. Hands too small, can't build a wall

3. Liberation, not deportation

4. All the walls have to go, Palestine to Mexico

5. No More Hate No More Fear!

6. No More Fear! No More Hate! America was never great!

7. Stop All Wars!

8. Hey, Hey, Ho, Ho! Fascism has got to go!

9. Democracy is under attack! What are we going to do? Stand up fight back!

10. Fund our future!

11. Jobs not war!

MAKE RACISTS AFRAID AGAIN

12. Tell us what Democracy looks like...this is what Democracy looks like!
13. No Wall No Ban!
14. 2,4,6,8 Stop the War Stop the Hate
15. When Fascists attack, We Fight Back!
16. We're Fired up. Won't take it no more!
17. There ain't no power like the power of the people, cause the power of the people don't stop. Say what?
18. Black, Latin, Asian, White. Standing up for Human Rights.
19. Not a nickel not a dime. Endless war is a crime!
20. Occupation is a Crime. Syria to Palestine.

MAKE RACISTS AFRAID AGAIN

21. Who's got the power? We've got the power! What kind of power? Voting power!

22. Union strong, union proud! Everybody say it loud!

23. Your lies and tricks will not divide; people are standing side by side!

24. Everyone together stand and fight. Education's a Human Right.

25. We Matter! We Care!

26. No Justice, No Peace!

27. Hey, hey stand up fight! Education's a human right!

28. No War, No KKK, No Fascist USA!

29. No More War! We Want Peace!

30. No More War! Fund our schools!

MAKE RACISTS AFRAID AGAIN

CONCLUSION

America is a multi-cultural nation and will never become an Ethno-State. But that will not stop Fascists and Neo-Nazis and White Supremacists and the Alt-Right from working towards that task. They are getting united. They are growing stronger. That is why you should now take it seriously how dire the situation is if you don't stand up to it. Endless war, poverty, crime, hate groups, hate crimes, hate speech, and divisive media, all work to create enmity and hate between people. It is up to humans to look past Nationalism. Nationalism led to over 200 million deaths in the 20th century and the mistakes of the 20th century should not be repeated in the 21st century. Humans should have learned from

MAKE RACISTS AFRAID AGAIN

the 20th century and the various social movements that arose to combat social problems and to combat Fascism. Humans are all of the same essence and in-fighting has never led to greater prosperity. In-fighting has only led to misery. Hate rips humans apart because it rips nations apart. Peace has never come at the end of a bayonet. The bayonet only has created more bayonets. But Fascism lives and dies with the bayonet. Humans are one long chain that are connected by each other's happiness and be each other's misery. Humans have to be there to support each other not only during times of happiness but more importantly during times of misery. By taking interest in all cultures, we ourselves become more cultured and

MAKE RACISTS AFRAID AGAIN

more understand of cultures other
than our own. No one is an island
and we do not live in caves. Humans
live in community, local and global.
By understanding and learning about
new cultures, we can communicate
and share with other cultures our
ideas and learn new ones from
theirs. Humans must not only
tolerate each other but they must
love and honor each other to achieve
unity. What can be more terrifying
than knowing that the media you
consume daily cannot be trusted.
That it is skewed. Not real. Fake.
Pretty scary in a democracy.
Whatever the Right Wing disagrees
with is labeled as Fake News. Even
news reporters that have no Left or
Right bearing, like the OC Weekly
reporter that was attacked in

MAKE RACISTS AFRAID AGAIN

Huntington Beach, have been labeled Fake News without a chance to report. Fascists movements share this element in common that they tend to label everything that they do not agree with as being Fake News. The Fake News scare in America triggered a mass panic in the media and among viewers about what is really fake news and what is not. It ultimately comes down to the credibility of the editor that makes that media produce news worthy material. All news is not news worthy unless it has social value to the community and to the viewers that are watching it. Much of what is called news today is re-reporting what another outlet has reported. News creation is costly, expensive, and time consuming. It is not easy or inexpensive to create news worthy material. The reason that news shows in the 1970's and 1980's was so valued is because a great deal of money was spent to generate the news. The current news shows regurgitate past news and call it breaking news. For it to be breaking news, your outlet has to be the one "breaking" or discovering and releasing the story. Fake News is news that attempts to portray and project and image rather than just reporting the facts. When extra words are put in to the story to push or project a viewpoint, that makes it commentary rather than actual news. Commentary is acceptable, but it is not news. News must be content that is purely factual without viewpoints added in that would push the listener/viewer to think a certain way. Not all media outlets can be trusted to be objective in their reporting of the news and that is why you should seek media outlets that are. Objectivity in reporting implies just reporting the facts in a non-biased manner that does not seek to project any viewpoint whatsoever. The media outlets on TV and on the Internet claim to be "fair and balanced" when in reality they are totally one-sided ideologically. The loss of objectivity in reporting and selective reporting are leading to the permanent loss of credible media sources for non-biased news. If the media outlets want to create greater viewership, then they have to be more objective and exhibit non-biased reporting. The Far Right

MAKE RACISTS AFRAID AGAIN

Media have been completely biased
and have not been balanced in their
reporting, despite their popularity.
Nationalism is sold as Patriotism,
when it has really been plain old
Fascism. Racism is institutional
despite being widespread in media
and society. The eradication of
Racism starts with self-examination
and introspection in the way we
conduct ourselves. How can we
eradicate Racism if we still any
traces of Racism from a falsely
conditioned past? The eradication of
Racism must start with self-
examination, introspection, and the
eradication of any all traces of
Racism from our lives and within
society.

MAKE RACISTS AFRAID AGAIN

**MIKAZUKI PUBLISHING HOUSE™
CATALOG**

1) 25 Principles of Martial Arts
2) 25 Principles of Strategy
3) American Antifa
4) Arctic Black Gold
5) Art of War
6) Back to Gold
7) Basketball Team Play Design Book
8) Beginner's Magicians Manual
9) Boxing Coloring Book
10) California's Next Century 2.0
11) Camping Survival Handbook
12) Captain Bligh's Voyage
13) Coming to America Handbook
14) Customer Sales Organizer
15) DIY Comic Book
16) DIY Comic Book Part II
17) Economic Collapse Survival Manual
18) Find The Ideal Husband
19) Football Play Design Book
20) Freakshow Los Angeles
21) Game Creation Manual
22) George Washington's Farewell Address
23) Hagakure
24) History of Aliens
25) I Dream in Haiku
26) Internet Connected World

27) Irish Republican Army Manual of Guerrilla Warfare
28) Japan History Coloring Book
29) John Locke's 2nd Treatise on Civil Government
30) Karate 360
31) Learning Magic
32) Living the Pirate Code
33) Magic as Science and Religion
34) Magicians Coloring Book
35) Make Racists Afraid Again
36) Master Password Organizer Handbook
37) Mikazuki Jujitsu Manual
38) Mikazuki Political Science Manual
39) MMA Coloring Book
40) Mythology Coloring Book
41) Native Americana
42) Ouija Board Enigma
43) Palloncino
44) Political Advertising Manual
45) Quotes Gone Wild
46) Rappers Rhyme Book
47) Self-Examination Diary
48) Shogun X the Last Immortal
49) Small Arms & Deep Pockets
50) Stories of a Street Performer
51) Storyboard Book
52) Swords & Sails

53) Tao Te Ching
54) The Adventures of Sherlock Holmes
55) The Art of Western Boxing
56) The Book of Five Rings
57) The Bribe Vibe
58) The Card Party
59) The History of Acid Tripping
60) The Man That Made the English Language
61) Tokiwa
62) T-Shirt Design Book
63) U.S. Army Anti-Guerrilla Warfare Manual
64) United Nations Charter
65) U.S. Military Boxing Manual
66) Van Carlton Detective Agency – Burgundy Diamond
67) William Shakespeare's Sonnet's
68) Words of King Darius
69) World War Water

MAKE RACISTS AFRAID AGAIN

NOTES

MAKE RACISTS AFRAID AGAIN

NOTES

MAKE RACISTS AFRAID AGAIN

NOTES

MAKE RACISTS AFRAID AGAIN

NOTES

MAKE RACISTS AFRAID AGAIN

NOTES

MAKE RACISTS AFRAID AGAIN

NOTES

MAKE RACISTS AFRAID AGAIN

NOTES

www.ingramcontent.com/pod-product-compliance
Lightning Source LLC
Chambersburg PA
CBHW072011290326
41934CB00007BA/1054